As I remember

As I remember

The Memoirs of
Edna Richmond Repard

Edited by Nila Repard

ISBN 978-1-329-65895-0
9 781329 658950

This book is dedicated to my father
Jerry (Jake) Repard

Prolog

I don't really feel like starting this but I don't think of any other use for this nice book that Jay[1] gave me for Christmas. Marilyn[2] suggested **I** write what I think are interesting stories that I remember. I think most others have heard them all and if they have, go no further. They are probably boring if you've heard them before.

This is written from memory of stories told to me by my grandmother, Clementine Louise Brown Adams and some of my own.

Edna Evalyn Richmond Repard

---

[1] Jay P. Repard (Edna's grandson)
[2] Marilyn Richmond Eddy (Edna's niece)

My grandmother's name was Clementine Louise Brown. She had a hectic childhood but she grew up with no serious problems. I believe she tried not to remember all the sad things that occurred. I, being the oldest grandchild, was privileged to hear stories that grandma was somewhat reluctant to tell. I've been told that I was a very inquisitive child and didn't hesitate to ask questions. Grandma made little effort to hide the fact she had no respect for her father who was Orin Brown. Her mother was Louisa Jurusha Doton. Her father deserted his family of nine young children, leaving their mother the responsibility of bringing them up.

Grandma was born in either Bradford or Rutherford Vermont on November 22, 1857, the seventh of nine children. Celia (b) 1848 (d) 1876, Charles (b) 1849 (d) 1863, Clara (b) 1851, Chauncey (b) 1852, Cora (b) 1854 (d) 1903, Chester (b) 1856, Clementine (b) 1857 (d) 1936, Jennie (b) 1859, Ella (b) 1861 (d) 1863.

There were few ways for a woman to earn enough for this job in those days. Louisa was forced to accept any help that presented itself. The older children went with relatives and friends and she took the three youngest into a lumber camp where she went to cook for the men who worked there.

When she was six years old Grandma was sent to Wisconsin in the care of the stage coach driver, to some friends or relatives who had volunteered to take her. She never really thought they wanted her but felt it their duty. They sent her back to her mother a year later. It apparently was not a happy time for her. Think of the effect such an experience would have on a six year old child. However it must have been a passing effect because Grandma was one of the most controlled personalities one ever knew.

Her oldest brother Charles enlisted in the Civil War on the northern side because he would be able to send $3.00 a month home to his mother to help with the younger children. He was fourteen years old but did not live long. He died in some Army camp of Typhoid fever.

When Grandma was about fifteen years old she was living with a Mr. and Mrs. William Scully. Mr. and Mrs. Levi Lord visited the

Scully home and as they had recently lost their only child, a girl about Grandma's age. They invited her to go to Phelps and live with them. She accepted although it meant severing her relationship with her siblings, such as it was. She was never able to return to Vermont, but in later years, a sister and two brothers visited her. She lived there with the Lords until she was eighteen and married my grandfather, Horace Winfield Scott Adams. Grandma was very frail when she married Grandpa. People referred to her as "Horace's ghost".

"Aunt Jane" as she called Mrs. Lord was very good to her. She bought her a purple taffeta dress. When Grandma displeased Aunt Jane the dress was taken from her clothes press and put in the spare room. When she returned to Aunt Jane's good graces the dress was returned.

There were other stories she told me. She remembered once her father threw a pot of hot tea at her mother as she held a baby. Another was that when her brothers Chauncey and Chester were teenagers they went up in the northern part of New Hampshire to work in the woods. Their father was living in Canada at the time and came across to the place they were the boys were working and collected their wages. They, of course, abandoned that job.

There are many stories that come creeping back into my mind. At the present time I live on memories. One time, Grandma was expecting a new baby, I never knew which one. Being human, she was quite despondent. Aunt Sarah was down to visit her and realized how depressed she was and said "Oh cheer up, diphtheria may come along before spring and take every last one of them".

That brought Grandma out of the doldrums. She knew Aunt Sarah loved every one of the children. Grandma said she could never have said which one of the children she would have wished not to have had. Grandma's children were; Ina Louella, (b) March 3, 1987 (d)April 29, 1964, Eva Elouisa (b) October 9, 1880 (d) December 5, 1973, Horace Seymour (b) October 20, 1881 (d) June 29, 1964, Albert Winfield (b) May 25, 1883 (d)April 3, 1951, Clementine May (b) March 26 1885 (d) April 21, 1951, Miller Wylie (b) July 16, 1886 (d) July 18 1963, Fred V. (b) July 27, 1889 (d) January 19, 1964, Arthur Lyndon (b) October 1, 1890 (d) September 18, 1939, Ethel Lamoine (b) May 6, 1892 (d) December 11, 1973, Lester Lord (b) April 8, 1899 (d) april18, 1979, Celia Violas (b) November 9, 1901 (d) August 22, 1982.

Grandma was pregnant thirteen times. Two of the babies died and one was still born. They were all buried in the south east corner of the grandparent's yard. That would be the place most of us remember as Uncle George and Aunt Ina's.

Aunt Ina was the second baby, weighing only two and a half pounds at birth. They didn't bath her, just wrapped her in cotton and laid her in a cigar box in a chair in front of the oven door. They fed her with a medicine dropper. She sure outgrew that two and half pounds.

She had her own brand of psychology. She said there were not two of them who responded to the same treatment. She told of spanking Aunt Ina when she reached the point she couldn't tolerate her, and later Aunt Ina would say "Thank you Mama for spanking me, I feel better now", but a good talking to could bring my mother back to good behavior. My mother told a lie once and had to wear a sign pinned to her back saying "This girl told a lie". Someone told her Grandfather, Winfield Scott Adams, who she adored. He came down and she took a seat in a chair and wouldn't get out. He kept asking her for things and she told him where he could get it but stayed put with her sign behind her.

I never understood her theory with Uncle Albert one time when he had erred. She took a small whip upstairs with Uncle Albert and sat down and told him he could choose. He could either whip her or she would whip him. Of course at first that was an easy decision, he chose the first. He struck her across the shoulders and it brought tears to her eyes. He saw the tears and threw down the whip and said "You can whip me all you want to; I'll never strike you again". I guess that accomplished the inward feeling she wanted to instill as that was the last of that. Uncle Albert was a very strong willed man and boy I suppose.

I heard from somewhere that Dr. Salisbury the vet in Clifton Springs said that there was never a person but Uncle Albert who he would want to help him with an angry sick animal as he knew Uncle Albert would never leave him to subdue the animal by himself.

My grandfather was not a tall man, rather stout in build. He had a great sense of humor. I spent a great deal of time at my grandparent's home as Celia and I were about the same age. Grandpa used to tease Grandma about her New England accent, things such as "dawg" for dog and "lawg" for log. Celia and I used to mimic Grandpa about his down east pronunciations. We were always on our good behavior when Aunt Sarah Buckingham was visiting. She had a habit of passing her teacup to Grandma at the end of the meal saying "just enough to rinse out my mouth". After she had left the table Celia and I tried the same thing but Grandma always told us the teapot didn't hold enough, meaning our mouths were too big. He had a horse "Old Rose" that had a heavy foretop. When my mother was quite young she sometimes did not comb her hair, just let it fall where it wanted to. Grandpa would call her "Old Rose". He was always interested in politics and especially in primaries. There being no TV or radio he always stayed at the election quarters until the votes were counted, he couldn't wait until the next morning.

There were three cobblestone houses east of Phelps. Grandma and Grandpa lived in the third one. Grandpa raised pure bred Morgan horses, broke them to drive and sent them to New York City to be sold to wealthy people to drive on their carriages. There were no Model T Fords at that time. Grandma used to say the horse had to have shoes whether the children did or not.

It was the children's job to carry salt once a week to the colts pasture on Vandemark's Flat. They were strictly forbidden to cross the foot bridge which had no side supports only horizontal slats to walk on. They were supposed to walk a little further to a regular bridge. The foot bridge was near a race; a large body of water held back to run a mill. Aunt May was with them one time when they decided to use the foot bridge. Aunt May fell in and was floating towards the mill wheel when Uncle Albert, jumped in. He couldn't swim, or at least he didn't know he could. He caught hold of her dress and pulled he to the bridge, the older ones pulled her out. Uncle Albert climbed out by himself. I think that was the last time they used the foot bridge.

It was at that house that Aunt Ethel was born. Dr. Vanderhoof was away; he had delivered all Grandma's babies and she refused to have another. An Old Danish lady, Mrs. Treadwell, who lived near them, delivered Aunt Ethel. Dr. Vanderhoof delivered all of grandma's children, except Aunt Ethel. Uncle Fred's middle name was V after Dr. Vanderhoof.

I've heard my mother tell that it was a wonder Aunt Ethel had any hair. The older girls used to curl her hair with a hot poker. Her hair was so light colored and they hadn't had a baby sister in a long time, so they loved to fix her up, as they would have liked to have been. Aunt May had red hair as Grandpa did; so did Uncle Seymour, Uncle Albert, and Lester.

My mother told me they always went up to her grandparents house for Thanksgiving. She said they had mashed potatoes and scalloped potatoes, turkey and roast pork, all sorts of vegetables, oyster soup and scalloped oysters, minced pie and pumpkin pie. The adults ate first, the children had to wait. She said it seemed like the adults took forever to eat. Then the kids ate until they were in misery from eating so much. Too bad it couldn't have been stretched out.

One year as they started to school at Melvin Hill, Uncle Albert didn't have shoes. The first day he wore an old pair of Aunt May's shoes that didn't fit. When he came home he took the shoes off and threw them away saying "I won't wear those cross-eyed things again". He went bare footed until cold weather when he got some shoes. It really wasn't such a hardship walking barefoot as Melvin Hill road was sandy. I remember when I walked home from Melvin Hill School I carried my shoes; I loved to squish the sand between my toes. I suppose that has all spoiled now, they have probably covered it with tar. Progress!!!

My big toe had a way of punching through my stockings. Grandpa always said he was going to cut the thumbs from some gloves and sew them on my stockings for an extension; he never got around to doing it. He had an old horse named Molly. She was blind and held her head to one side. We could always tell it was Grandpa coming when they were quite a way off by the way Molly held her head. Grandpa never tied old Molly when he came. One evening Leonard got in the buggy and picked up the lines and Molly started. She was blind so couldn't see where she was going and Leonard didn't know how to steer. Someone found him across the road crying. Molly had gone between a pole and a tree but it was too narrow for the buggy so Molly stopped.

When Leonard was about three my mother always put a piece of newspaper under his plate when we went to Grandma's. One day Grandma and Grandpa came to our house for supper so Leonard thought he would return the compliment and put papers under their plates. My mother was going to remove the paper but Grandma persuaded her to leave it as he had fixed it.

Grandma told me her mother's name was Doton, her mother's name was Vaughn and her mother's name was Le Baron. I remember how important I felt for a short time as I understood the name Le Baron was a French nobility name. Grandma let me enjoy my importance for a time then told me Le Baron meant the farmer. I was somewhat wilted.

Grandpa entered a depressed period of his life when he was in his 50's. He must have been in his 50's because Uncle Miller, Uncle Fred, and Uncle Arthur were single at the time. They pooled their money, raising $1000.00 and bought the place on South Wayne St in Phelps NY for their parents and the youngest three children. That was the place my grandparents lived out their lives in. Grandpa worked by the day after they moved over to the South Wayne St home. I lived there a while and went to school; in fact my parents lived there also between moves of which there were many.

Times were hard for Grandma and Grandpa. All the children did all they could to help taxes were not as hard to face and food was not as expensive. He kept one red cow, Grandma made their butter. She always had a garden called the "Pat Lot" and an apple orchard. Why it was called the Pat Lot I never knew. It's a wonder I never asked. My mother said they got one orange a year at Christmas.

Grandpa had two sisters Sarah and Ella. Sarah was a Civil War widow getting along on a very small pension, $3.00 to start it went up to $9.00 before she died. She never had to provide for herself as she owned a small farm and lived with her parents after her husband died. She took care of her invalid mother, saving her entire pension. Aunt Sarah came to live with Aunt Ina around 1916 or 17. She was very frail requiring quite a bit of care. Everyone who knew Aunt Sarah loved her. Her sister Aunt Ella died in 1918, Aunt Sarah in 1919, and Grandpa in 1920. My grandfather had eaten a very hearty dinner at noon and it was a very hot day. It was August 6, 1920 and they were cutting barley the day he died. The doctor said he had acute indigestion which boiled down in today's diagnostic language would be a heart attack.

Aunt Ina lived at her grandparents' home as she grew up, to help Aunt Sarah. Although they always had a hired girl, Aunt Sarah was a very apprehensive person, she worried about everything thus she transferred that characteristic to Aunt Ina. I don't think anyone ever went to Phelps that Aunt Ina didn't call out "Watch the cars" meaning the Lehigh Railroad. The year I was sixteen I helped Aunt Ina as she was caring for Aunt Sarah that year, Aunt Ina's son Jimmy always called me the "hired girl". Jimmy slept in the little room at the head of the front stairs. I slept in the spare room. Jimmy got interested in reading a book called "Her Father's Daughter" by Gene Stratton Porter (a very proper book). He was reading in bed with a lamp when his mother called upstairs about 8 o'clock and said to put out the light. He said "can't I finish this chapter". Aunt Ina, thinking he was reading the bible said he could. Thereafter when he and I drove the horse and buggy to Phelps for groceries he always said "Let me forcibly invite you to proceed to your destination" which was a phrase used in that book. He also would ask me to compound a cake" and "freeze a custard". I earned $3.00 a week while I was there and saved it all and bought a winter coat. That was the year I went into training. I wore that coat long after I was married.

The year Aunt Sarah died she left a will leaving $7000.00 to Grandpa. One of Aunt Ella's daughters tried to break the will by saying Aunt Sarah was of unsound mind. I was seventeen at the time and was at Grandpa's house when the lawyer, Leon Van Dusen, came to talk to him. I do not claim any outstanding wisdom but I told the lawyer Aunt Sarah always sent me a birthday card on April 20th. That year it was a day late, but she had written on the card she realized she was late in sending it but had just over looked it. The Lawyer wanted that card and I produced it. He took me and the card to the Surrogate Office in Canandaigua, my first trip to Canandaigua, and put me on the stand to verify I had received this card from Aunt Sarah. It convinced the Judge that Aunt Sarah's mind was OK and let the will stand. Grandpa didn't live long to enjoy the release from the tension he had felt for a long time, but Grandma had it to use for the sixteen years she survived his death. She wasn't used to having much money to spend and was a good manager and $7000.00 was a lot more back in 1920 than it would be now.

Grandma bonded her eleven children with love that lasted throughout their lives. She was one of the best adjusted people I ever knew. I dearly loved her and wish the younger cousins could have known her as I did.

After Grandpa died my father was back on the railroad as a carpenter so Mom, Esther, and Leonard moved from Honeoye Falls to Grandma's so she wouldn't be alone

Grandma lost one eye; she never had an artificial eye, just a frosted lens in her glasses. She died after having a gall bladder operation in Clifton Springs Spa Sanitarium. It seemed ironic that her six sons were there as she passed out of her life. As they left the Sanitarium the photographer's window across the street had Grandma's picture displayed for Mother's Day. Mr. Case, the photographer, was a family friend.

My mother liked to work outdoors and when they were drawing hay she and Uncle Seymour loaded the wagon while Uncle Albert and Grandpa pitched it on. Uncle Seymour very strongly disapproved of girls driving horses. If my mother wanted to pick a fight she would manage to grab the lines and drive to the next Haycock. It seemed that was about the only thing they disagreed on.

There used to be a watering trough a little way up the road where Grandma and Grandpa lived that was at the edge of the lane. The cows drank from one side and the other was used by people driving past and would stop and let the horses get a drink. Uncle Seymour was known for getting his words mixed up. One time when he came to the barn he took the bits out of the horses' mouths and let them go to the watering trough by themselves. He had forgotten to remove the checks and the horses couldn't get their heads down so he ran out to the trough to uncheck them. When he came back he said "Ben the water all over my foot spilt".

Seymour · Eva

As I remember, Aunt May came to our house on West Main St in Phelps and had her first baby who lived only a short time. Grandma came to help my mother.

It was my privilege to sleep with Grandma when she was at our house. It was at this time I was told most of these stories. I always cherished them but wonder if I should write about them, but see no reason why the other grandchildren shouldn't know what a wonderful grandmother we had. Aunt Ina used to say she sometimes dreaded to learn I was coming to visit her as I asked so many questions. She couldn't have minded too much as I spent a lot of time at Aunt Ina's and Uncle George's. I loved them both.

My mother and father worked very hard all their lives. I don't remember them ever taking a vacation with each other except the one time Esther took them down to Helen's. My father did go on a fishing trip on Lake Huron with some railroad friends. He was gone less than a week. My mother's vacations were when she would go somewhere to help someone who needed a little extra help. Like when Aunt Ethel came home with Edwin, she was very nervous and afraid she wouldn't do things right for him. Mom took Leonard and went to help Aunt Ethel until she got used to caring for a new baby. It was there that Leonard was watching them giving Edwin a bath. He wanted to say something nice to Aunt Ethel and said "He looks like a little red man". It made Aunt Ethel laugh and that was what they were aiming to do at that point, to ease the tension Aunt Ethel was dealing with.

My parents Edward and Eva were married June 6, 1900. They worked for his parents the first year. She did house work as Grandma Richmond was crippled with arthritis. The second year they moved to the Sanitarium Farm in Clifton Springs.

In the early spring of 1903 they moved to Eagle Street, Phelps. I was born there April 20, 1903. He worked on the Lehigh Railroad He walked a certain section of track after each train passed. He worked at night. In August they moved to a house on Mill Street. The rent of the house in those days was $6.00 a month and his wages were $1.17 a night.

In 1905 they moved to a farm that Aunt Sarah Buckingham owned. It was on Fort Hill Road in Phelps. Esther was born there May 27, 1905. In 1907 they moved to the Ben Westfall farm east of Phelps. There was more land there. Alvin was born there June 30, 1907 (and died July 1, 1907). The next place they bought was on West Main Street Phelps. Dad was Village Constable and worked as a carpenter for Joel Caves.

In 1912 they sold the house on West Main Street Phelps and moved to 31 Lyceum Street Geneva. We stayed there only one month. They bought the farm on Melvin Hill from Charles Donnely in the spring of 1912. Leonard was born there September 8, 1912. I was nine when we moved to Melvin Hill. I soon discovered two very interesting ladies who lived next to us; at least they were very interesting to me. They were Mary and Laurie Carpenter, both old maids and graduates of Elmira College for Women. I'm not sure but I think at one time they taught school. They sure taught me a lot, and I was very eager to learn. They allowed me to do things I'm sure my mother would never have allowed.

Laurie was bedridden and terribly overweight, I never knew why she was bedridden, I wonder why I never asked. I was never a good housekeeper but realized at that young age that Mary was not either. I was allowed to do many thinks for Laurie and wonder if that was the beginning of my desire to become a nurse. There was an iron pole through the floor at the head of Laurie's bed. There was a crane like apparatus that swung over the bed. It had very heavy straps attached. I could and did roll Laurie over on her side and put a canvas partway under her, then rolled her back and pulled the canvas through. Then I hooked the straps to each corner and with a crank, pulled Laurie over her wheel chair and took her to any part of the house she wanted to go. There was a porch at each end of the front of the house but no railing so I never remember that she ever got outdoors.

Mary used to go for elderberries and I went with her. She brought home the berries and laid newspaper on Laurie's bed and Laurie picked out the stems. You can imagine what the bed looked like after the elderberries rolled around, and the color of Laurie's hands. But a little color didn't bother anyone.

They had a horse named John. Once a week Mary and, usually, I went to Phelps to deliver butter. I often wonder about the people who bought the butter as Mary's hair was always straggly and I would imagine a hair could easily slip into the butter. I never heard any complaints. She always took a paring knife to cut a switch along the road to urge John along. I remember watching Mary work the butter. She used several pails of water to wash the buttermilk out. She always worked the butter ladle towards her, she said if you pushed it away you would break some veins in the butter and it would poison you. I never heard anyone else with that idea but I believed it.

There was an old man who lived there and did what farm work was done, his name was Royal Phelps. I went to the barn once. They had about twenty very skinny cows. I doubt if Mr. Phelps ever cleaned the barn.

Mary went to an alumni convention in Elmira and was to be gone for two days. She must have convinced my mother in some way that I was capable of staying with Laurie. Mr. Phelps did his own cooking. I might have been eleven or twelve then, I slept on the couch in the room with Laurie. Many additional rudiments of nursing were learned years later.

There was a small stream of water between the house and barn. Wild peppermint and spearmint grew on the banks of the stream. I ate plenty of those leaves. I wonder how I grew up so healthy, I still wonder if all this sterilizing is really necessary.

I don't think my mother ever worried too much about me. She probably knew if I wasn't home I was at Carpenters. We moved away from Melvin Hill when I was thirteen. It was the happiest place I ever lived and we lived in many different places. I never did hear what happened to those old ladies.

He tried many ways to increase his income. He bought a threshing machine and a saw mill. He always enjoyed working with wood in one way or another.

He then sold the farm to a man from Naples. We moved to Syracuse, 114 Blust Street, Eastwood. He worked for a Mr. Rice at various jobs. The rent on that house was $25.00 a month and they felt they couldn't afford that much so we moved to 300 White Ave, Onandoga Valley. I had my thirteenth birthday when we lived in Onandaga Valley.

I remember a man coming to the door with a milk can and dipper. Mom took a basin out and got as much milk as she needed at $.07 a quart. It was raw milk but we thrived on it. In fact our own children were brought up on raw milk. Helen use to take a cup to the barn and catch a cup full as Ed put the milk through a strainer into the cans. Later, of course, everyone had milk tanks. Mary Ellen Sullivan use to love to carry the milker into the milkhouse and strain it into the tank when they were visiting us.

Evelyn and Elaine Richmond told me that when they were younger they didn't like Rich Sullivan because he said he was going to take all the cows home to Haverstraw with him. They couldn't imagine the place without cows. Rich had no place to keep the cows but thought he could keep them in the basement of the Methodist church next door. I imagine Rich knew he could tease the girls. The man who bought the Melvin Hill farm apparently was displeased with his purchase so the farm came back to father.

We moved back to the farm and stayed until he sold it to Charlie Dhalle. We moved to a house on Clifton Street in Phelps. He was then working for the BR&P Railroad out of Rochester. Shortly they transferred him to DuBois, PA. We lived at 525 First Street there. He was working on cars for carpenter gangs to live in and knew they were infested with bedbugs. So when he was notified he would be going out in these cars, he quit.

He went to Phelps to Aunt Kate Beale's funeral and while there he found a job in Victor working for a farmer named Hiram Boughton. We stayed there a year and then moved to York Street, Honeoye Falls where he worked in a flour mill. They then bought a house on Railroad Ave in Honeoye Falls and worked for an oil company delivering oil with a tank wagon and horses as far away as Allen's Hill.

Later he went back to the Railroad. In 1920 Grandpa Adams died and they rented the house on Railroad Ave. and moved to Phelps with Grandma. In 1922 He and Ed Repard bought the Wheeler Station Rd. farm in Holcomb where he died April 25, 1962. She died December 5, 1973. Ed Repard died December 9, 1979. Helen, Jim, Roger, Nancy, and Leonard Colf were all born here.

Mom also went to Phelps to help Grandma when Lester had an ear infection. We lived in Honeoye Falls at the time. Leonard came down with the chicken pox and I was cautioned to keep him in bed and warm. He learned the multiplication tables by counting off the squares in the ceiling paper as he lay on the couch.

In March of 1945 we had a sad catastrophe. Leonard and Lillian's oldest son David was killed at the age of seven. I'll never forget the blow I felt when Ed told me when he came after me that night. Helen was home at the time but could not wait for the funeral as she had joined the Army and had to leave for Texas.

Mom loved everyone and especially enjoyed company. On Saturdays she would bake all morning in case someone should come on Sunday. She baked bread at home and Ed Repard took her to Canandaigua two times a week to sell it to regular customers. She never had a license I can imagine how quick she would have been run out of business now days.

After Dad went back to work on the railroad she raked hay for Ed, pulled beets and carrots, and raised all kinds of poultry; chickens, ducks, geese, and turkeys to sell in the fall especially for Christmas time. Of course I was supposed to be helping but as I think of it now I didn't do as much as I could have done to have made her life happier, not that she ever seemed unhappy. She used to enjoy playing checkers with Nila. When Nila saw she was going to get beat she suggested they change the rules. That pleased Grandma. My mother worked very hard all her life yet lived to be 93 years old. My father hardly ever missed a day of work and was never out of a job. If he couldn't find a job he would cut wood and sell it. He built a number of barns, hired men who needed work badly and sort of ruled them with an iron hand. He ran his own little welfare corporation. For instance one man had not worked for three days. Dad stopped at the corner and told him, his vacation was over and for him to be on the corner at 6:30 AM the next morning, The man was there. He once took him home and his wife found he had no money left from his pay check. The wife began to cry as their son had no shoes to wear to school the next week. Dad took her and the son to Canandaigua in his old International truck and got the shoes that were needed.

He had two suits at one time, there was a family who had a fire and lost everything. One morning Dad was ready to leave for work and went back upstairs. When he came down he had the gray suit rolled up in a small roll under his arm. Mom asked what he was going to do with it and he told her he was giving it to the father since he had no use for two suits.

Violet Eddy told me that she and Lynn Steele were talking about dad one day. Lynn said it was too bad there were no more Ed Richmonds around. At the last of his working years Dad worked at the Bennett's farms. His check was much less than it had been when he was doing real carpenter work. My mother asked him why he worked for such a small amount and he said "Because I'm not worth more". I have always been very proud of both my parents and only wish I can be remembered with as much love as they are.

In June 1920 I finished my 2nd year of High School in Honeoye Falls. You only needed 17 credits to enter Nursing School, 34 to graduate. I wanted to be a nurse; my mother was very much against it. At that time nursing was very low on the list of respectability. I didn't know, nor care. She went with me to Dr. Marlatt's office on Monroe St to try to have him convince me to go back to school. Instead he compromised by getting me a job at the Monroe County Hospital on South Ave. He, being a friend of the head of the County Poor Department, went to them (I've forgotten their name) and the Supervisor's wife had me room with them in their private quarters at the Almshouse. It was a beautiful home with hot and cold water in the room. The nurse's home was across the street and was not a very nice place.

Each Monday AM we'd get a slip of paper telling us when we were to work that week. First I worked in the Nursery where children were kept until adopted. There were seven cribs. The only one adopted while I was there was a little blonde boy 14 months old who could only walk around his crib as he was never out of it. I remember I dressed him ready to be taken to the Court House to meet his new parents.

There were three morphadite (Down's syndrome) children. Catherine, age 5, was not supposed to be out of her crib but did manage to climb out. She was very mean to the other babies, pulling their hair and hitting their hands etc. The nursery, was directly off a large ward of elderly women, some bedridden, some able to get around. There was one known as Grandma Higgins who had Catherine brought in on her bed and entertained her by cutting out pictures, otherwise, Catherine had to be tied to the side of the bed to protect the other babies. Catherine stayed days at a time with Grandma Higgins. Imagine allowing that today. I don't know what would be done to Catherine nowadays, very likely sent to an institution like Newark, although. I would say she was mentally bright.

One day someone came and told me to go upstairs to the delivery room, a woman was giving birth. I got there and found no one else but the patient. I panicked, at 14 I had been with Aunt May when Earl was born but hardly realized what was going on. I left and found an R.N. and asked her to come and tell me what to do. I think someone did arrive and took over. That was the first baby I saw born and it was dead. I didn't seem to upset the mother.

Soon I was told by the Monday AM slip to go to Detention. I didn't even know where it was. I was sent down in the basement were there was a ward with 17 beds and 7 cells. There was an elderly lady, there who knew what she was doing, I surely didn't.

I found that as soon as they found a patient upstairs that was ready to pass away, they brought them downstairs to detention. I soon found out how to "lay out" patients after death. One week there were seven. This was supposed to make me discouraged with nursing and return to school, it didn't.

I learned to give a hypo on an old lady who was comatose. An R.N. came down and had me practice on that poor old woman's arm, I can't say how many times. I was so eager to learn it didn't bother me a bit.

I remember at supper time an orderly brought a large tray in and set it on a large table at the end of the room. 17 cups of tea with a slice of bread over the top of each cup was their supper. In the cells there were mentally disturbed patients, one who was so edematous we didn't shut her door as she couldn't possible get through the door.

Each patient who was destined for the cells had to have a tub bath. Her clothes were thrown in a "hog's head" barrel of disinfectant were they disintegrated. Sometimes that bath was quite a tussle. On Mrs. Barnes day off I was alone; there was an old lady who had come to America from Switzerland who was in misery on one of those days. I was alone, she begged me to give her an enema. She supervised the proceedings as I had never had any experience with enemas. I was 100% perplexed to find her uterus on a pillow, entirely out of her body but attached by something resembling an umbilical cord. She was very thankful to me for giving, with her assistance, the enema. About two days later the nurse supervisor, who never left the office, had heard that I had given that enema. She called me into a supply room and told me I had committed a grade "A" sin by giving an enema without a doctor's order and never do such a thing again. I never did, there. This all occurred in a little over a month as on August 6 I got a phone call that my grandfather had died. I immediately went to pieces and resigned as on September 1st I had been accepted at Park Ave Hospital nurses training.

It was right after WWI, they were short of nurses, I was not 18 but they accepted me. I went home, which was Phelps. I met Ed Repard at my Grandfather's funeral, but did go to Park Ave. Hospital September 1st where I was the first student to arrive for the new class making me President of the class. The next day Vivian Arnold age 36 came, then Mable Mohan, Ruth Mae Naughton, and Helen Jenkins who was the only one to finish training.

There were 17 student nurses in the entire school, one Superintendant of Nurses (R.N.) Mrs. Morris, one House Physician Dr. Merle, and one Operating Room Supervisor an R.N. The senior nurses supervised the lower two classes. I think I remember most of the other students. In the senior class there was Sophia Colburn in her late 20's, Betty Leathersich in her late 20's, Mable Smith might have been 30, Katherine Hollister somewhere between 25 and 35, died before graduation, Katherine Tracey a confirmed old maid, that's only five, there must have been more. In the intermediate class was Louise Knight, Thelma Jones, and Mildred Walton and the five I remember from the class I was in.

Our class was in the attic, I believe there were eight cots in the room, across the hall was a two bed room where Jones and Walton roomed. Knight slept in the two bed room on the second floor. After Hollister died there were some changes. I was transferred to the second floor which was no favor to me, my new roommate was a hateful personality and all the seven snickered when I was moved down there. We had one window. It was May and very warm, if I raised the window 2" she would get out her umbrella to shield her head from a draft. Miss Denniston, the OR Supervisor, had a single room on the second floor.

In the mean time I began to have back aches that I was foolish enough to complain about. I should have just grinned and bore that. I was treated like a child. To pass away the time once I took my apron and bib down stairs and cold starched them as they came back from the laundry very limp. I was reported by someone and the laundress was very angry with me. Some of the others got a laugh at my discomfort over the drawing out I got about that. They also got a lot of fun out of my getting to room with my roommate. One night I couldn't lay still and she yelled at me to lay still. That night Miss Denniston was away so I took my sheet and pillow in her room, spread the sheet over her spread and used my own pillow and slept in there. That, of course, was a very sinful thing to have done.

The house was a double house on Morningside Park a block away from the hospital. After I got my cap and bib, three months, I was put on senior duty with no supervision over Louis Knight, who got the medical floor. It, by the way, was at night and I had to walk one block on Brunswick St. It so happened Louise and I were good friends. She did not appear to resent me as I feel she might rightfully have done. I got by that OK. We had two hours off each day for classes, if, on night duty you got up for classes.

Then I was sent to Maternity on the 4th floor. I was lucky; my first patient was a former graduate of that school and directed me from the delivery table, which I was forever grateful. I had all the O.B. patients I needed to graduate before I was sent to the third floor which was usually the junior duty before Medical. I never knew the reason they changed the routine.

We were paid a stipend of $7.00 a

Edna Richmond Rebhard.

29

month but had to pay for any breakage we caused. On second floor once I started out of the Medicine room with a tray of thermometers and caught my sleeve on the latch on the door, breaking seven thermometers at .75 each. At that time we all wore cotton stockings which were .25 a pair. High shoes laced to mid calf, white from May 1st to November 1st then black shoes. Woe be unto anyone who did not have the right colored shoes and stockings at the right date because you held up everyone until you got in line. You were very unpopular if you were the odd one. At that time money was very scarce as it was for a long time and my mother sent me $1.00 and a letter cautioning me to be very careful. I believe I saved that dollar and had my shoes in time; otherwise the $7.00 a month bought my stockings. I learned to darn the toes of my stockings making them last longer.

Ed Repard was working on the Railroad with my father at the time. He used to walk over and visit me once in a while. I went to two movies during the time I spent there. My father came and took me and Louise Knight. They didn't want me walking the streets in Rochester. Louise went home with me a week and then we had one together. After Louise graduated she became O.R. nurse at the new Monroe County Hospital and never worked anywhere else. Her home was in Canada.

Then in November I had two weeks' vacation in 1921. I went home decidedly unhappy, I did not return. I should have because I immediately started taking care of maternity cases at home. First was Blanch White Hunt, then Alice Lake Crouch.

In February 1922 Ed and I were married. I didn't work after that until Roger was about four years old. My mother took care of both boys, Jim and Rod. I took O.B. cases, mostly for Dr. Howard. I did nursing, housework, everything for $21.00 a week, 24 hours a day. We needed the money so badly. I also had cases for Dr. Clapper and Dr Harry Smith. I had some medical cases also, once in a while, I had 12 hour duty. Ed was not happy with me being away but there seemed to be no other way. My father went back to the railroad, later did general carpentry work. Ed worked the farm, and when the boys were off enough they helped him.

On one occasion I was taking care of an elderly lady everyone called "Aunt Hattie" her husband was "Uncle Charlie". He asked me all sorts of personal questions. If I went home for a few hours he came after me in horse and buggy. He waved at every house, I asked him who he was waving at and he wouldn't want anyone who saw him to think he was "stuck up". His brother was a pharmacist, owned a drug store in Canandaigua. His wife was the former Elizabeth Bacon. She was high society. She came up to Bristol every Monday A.M., her chauffeur drove for her. She bossed poor Uncle Charlie around unmercifully. I had been there three weeks and she asked me if I had been paid. I told her no, she gave Uncle Charlie his instructions that he was to pay me. In the mean time he had noticed Ed had a new mowing machine and he asked me if it was paid for and how much it cost. I told him no he had paid for it with a note and it was $90.00. He wrote a check for $90.00 and left it on his desk were I had to see it every time I went through the room. On Monday A.M. when he saw "Aunt Lizzy" coming he hurried in and gave me the check. He told me to pay that note for the mowing machine. I gave it to Ed, I don't know if he paid the note until it was due.

Going back to training days, I took my dietetic training at the old Mechanics Institute downtown, it later became R.I.T. We went at night; the street car line on Park Avenue was the crookedist ride anyone ever took. We could hardly stay in the seats. The Motorman on that route was Leon Lathrop who was from Phelps. It was usually a very hilarious trip. We never learned much at that class as we were taught fundamentals at class in the nurse's home. We had different M.D.'s as teachers Dr. Jennings from Macedon, taught anatomy, Dr. Carrol taught ears, nose and throat. I was not an excellent student but did pass the final exam with a 99 in his class. I think the fact that I was younger than the others and felt out of place at their evening meeting, I spent the time studying. If I hadn't spent the time studying I wouldn't have even passed most of the exams. I was never a "student". Dr. Chaffee was the Monroe County Bacteriologist taught us Bacteriology. He was in the Nursery one day as I was bathing babies. He told me "always keep the baby's belly covered, even when bathing." He made no explanation but that remark always stayed in my mind. My mind has always had the ability to retain unimportant things.

The babies I helped deliver are now either parents or grandparents. I took care of Leona Webb when Glen was born. Her only other child was 17 at the time Glen was born, Dr. Clapper had to come from Victor with horse and buggy. He said it was a beautiful moonlit night so he didn't hurry, thinking he had plenty of time. Mae Webb had come and got me in the evening and by 10:30 P.M. Glenn arrived. It was the first time I delivered a baby without a doctor. I cut the cord in two places far apart and wrapped the baby in a blanket and put him in a basket made ready for him. The doctor arrived wanting to know where the baby was. He was surprised and then delivered the placenta.

Winfield Adams

Elouisa Miller Adams

34

Aunt Clara + Mother

35

Ina Adams Richmond

Fred Adams

Lester Adams

Arthur Adams

Ed   Ed   Edna   Mother Miller Loretta

41

Horace & Clementine Adams
Great, Grandparents

Uncle Albert   Lloyd-   Aunt Nellie

Desta   Merton

45

Marion + Lester

York St, Honeoye Falls

52

The very next case was the birth of Lois Northrup. They called Dr. Smith, who was out in the middle of Canandaigua Lake on his yacht. So I did his job for him. By this time I was not as nervous. I then told Dr. Howard I would call him a month ahead of time if need be.

The next was a baby for Esther and Carl Stell on the Middle Cheshire Rd. This was the second case I had been with them. It was their fifth child, eventually they had ten. She was diabetic and was blind later in life. Dr. Howard, however, did not arrive before the baby that time. I asked Carl to bring a pan of water with disinfectant, he did bring a huge pan of water and I'm sure added a whole bottle of Lysol. All I needed was enough to cover a pair of scissors and a piece of string. Middle Cheshire Rd. was not improved; Dr. Howard drove a Model T Ford which had to come in hub deep mud. When he came he saw this pan on the floor and asked me if I had been washing my feet. I think those were the only three cases I didn't get the doctor there in time.

I took care of Mrs. Weldon Kershaw who lived in the Gardener's house at Sonnenberg. There was a little girl, six years old, Elaine, who cried a little when her mother died but said "There's just one thing about it, I'm going to have some high heels." Poor little kid, she didn't understand what was happening to her at the time.

I took care of Mrs. Hickox on Adelaide Ave. She had cancer. I took care of her days and Bobby Reed took nights.

Dr. Brockmyre sent for me to take care of Barney Spike in Hopewell. He cautioned me not to move him at any time. He had a clot in the femoral artery, extremely painful. He died with all his clothes on. The doctor didn't even want us to cut them off. I was only there a night and part of a day. I stayed and watched Kennedy's prepare his body for burial.

I also took care of Joe Kaveny on Pearl St. He was also Dr. Brockmyre's patient. I was there more than a week with no time off to sleep. I was so tired when I got home I had a nightmare that night. I took Ed by the shoulders and said "Ed Repard, what do you think you're doing?" I was seeing him fight for breath as Mr. Kaveny had been doing.

One year, in May, I went to East Bloomfield to take care of Mr. Wright who lived in the large white house opposite Brush and Violet Eddy's home, later Stuart and Margaret Caves lived there. Mr. Wright was 90 years old and had a broken hip. He was a very pleasant dispositioned man with a keen sense of humor, but very stubborn in having his own way. He was in a double bed, on a feather bed and wore a long night shirt. He was a tall man but not heavy. The worse part of his care was getting him on a bed pan. As I remember he didn't complain of pain. He used a urinal so never wet the bed. He refused a bath, didn't want his bed changed (flannel sheets) and maintained his night shirt didn't need changing because he never sweat. His housekeeper, Mrs. Norton, advised me to let him have his own way. I could turn him off his back by using a pillow to bolster him on his side once in a while. He always chewed each mouthful of food twenty times, even his milk. We were hours getting his meals into him. He had been a manufacturer of furniture when he was younger. He loved daring me to find hiding places he had built in furniture and the house. There was one in the closet off his room. There were several shelves at one end; the one at about knee height had a slanted compartment even with the shelf's edge and slanting down to about four inches in the back. It had a trick opening which let down from the front edge. Another was under the front stairway. A shelf the whole length of, about, the fifth stair could be removed and the panel in back of the shelf could be pushed to one side revealing a space under the lower stairs. His bedposts were topped with what looked like pineapples. The tops of these pineapples could be unscrewed to hold small amounts of valuables. I asked him why he was letting me know of these places, was it so he could accuse me of robbing him if he ever lost anything? He said, "No, just to prove that I would be a very poor burglar, as he had to tell me about each one." I was only there two weeks as some relative came and took him somewhere near Syracuse by ambulance.

I worked at the Ontario County Home in 1935 for $50.00 a month and maintenance. I could have the kids, one at a time, come on weekends. Jim must have been 12, Roger 10. During Jim's visits he learned to play pool. The old men enjoyed him as he learned real fast. They thought it was because they were good teachers. Roger and Caroline Buck, who was about his age, played together. Helen came, but stayed with Jean Noble at the Main house. They both became nurses, married doctors, but I don't think they ever carried their friendship any further. Ed came several weekends and stayed to Sunday dinner. I think he enjoyed those weekends. Everyone else had their families living there. I only stayed there a year that time.

I went back there in 1959 and worked until I was 70 years old. The State required you to retire at 70, but Mrs. Mellor got an extension of two years for me. However, I went home one A.M. and found my mother on the floor. She had slipped when getting on the commode. I immediately made up my mind I wouldn't be able to leave her anymore, so I phoned Mrs. Mellor that I wouldn't be able to work any longer. She accepted it most graciously; the County surely treated me more than fairly at that time. That was in March and Mom lived until December. Mrs. Mellor loaned me a bed and a lift which no one used there. We had a doctor from Victor come a couple of times. Dick Sullivan, Helen's husband, sent prescriptions for medicines for both Mom and Ed. The doctor came after Mom died; I said maybe I should have put her in a hospital. He said no, he was sure she had better care at home, that made me feel good. Ed was happy when I quit, I hadn't realized how he had felt responsible for Mom, especially when she fell and he hadn't heard her.

In 1935 Welfare was just starting. Before that each town had a Supervisor of the Poor, Mr. Welch was overseer of the poor for years in Phelps or people who needed help had to accept help from friends and neighbors. I remember when Lewis Main, a very special lifelong friend of my father had a problem with his hip. He couldn't move without a great deal of pain. They had four children and he was unable to work. They needed help. My father took a paper around to people he knew and asked for contributions. If they felt they could, they signed their names and the amount they gave. Some small other large amounts. I think $5.00 was a large amount. He finished up with $100.00 and took it to them. It was a fortune to them at the time. Some people gave a bushel of potatoes, others gave other food items. It went on for some time until someone convinced Mr. Main to go to the Sanitarium in Clifton Springs.

Once there, the doctor asked him if he had lain on his stomach lately. Mr. Main told him it had been impossible. The doctor asked him to get on the table on his stomach. He made an attempt to, got on his knees and chest but couldn't get way down. The doctor stepped out from behind a curtain and pushed on the small of his back and forced him down. I guess it was very painful, but his hip snapped back in place. He had dislocated the hip when he tipped over on a load of hay. He slowly became better and last I remember him he was running a threshing machine. This all happened before I was nine years old. I just remember the story being told.

I started out to tell of the time that Welfare was started. The Welfare Supervisor's headquarters where in the Masonic Hall in back of the Court House in Canandaigua. His family lived in the house at the "Poor Farm" in Hopewell. The County Home, at that time, had no elevator; all trays for the sick women were carried up stairs by the women who could just about make it up the stairs. Most of these women had been inmates of Newark Institution for feeble minds. The sick women were on the second floor at one end, the men who couldn't make it to the dining room were on the first floor at the other end of the building. We had some weird characters. There was Eva Vanderlyke, from Phelps, she walked very much like I do now, bent over, her hair always wild, as mine would be if I didn't have a perm. I was giving Eva a bath one day and she told me she had done dirtier work than she did at the time and was washed less for it. I tried and think I managed to give each woman a bed bath a week. I was the only nurse with one orderly, Carl Smith, to care for the entire number of men and women there. Some of the women who could get around and help themselves a little got tub baths. Things were a lot different when I went back there in 1959. There was an elevator, patients needing more supervision where all on the second floor, and there were many more people working. At first I was alone with one attendant. He was an alcoholic and I didn't see him until 5:00 A.M. Mrs. Dewey had told me I need not consider the care of the men my responsibility. Later I had two people working with me, and Howard King, an L.P.N., who was very good, took care of the men. No one had to worry about any unkind tricks by the attendant losing his temper. On his nights off it was a different story. I didn't work days but I knew many things that happened in the day that wouldn't have been tolerated if I had been responsible.

I worked the whole building alone many nights because the relief attendants were intoxicated. One orderly walked out at midnight one time, saying nothing. I phoned Mr. Dewey to tell him he had left. Mr. Dewey called him at home and asked his reason for leaving. The orderly said he wouldn't work with that damned substitute nurse. She was only working that shift as substitute for someone who was off. Mr. Dewey told him he better come back and apologize to Mrs. Repard. He said "To hell with Mrs. Repard and the whole place". He was so drunk it was really a relief to have him gone.

There was another aid who did anything she thought of to make a patient uncomfortable. She and I had many battles a 7:00 A.M. when she arrived on duty and I was leaving. One evening Mr. Dewey came over and asked if I would consider working with her. I thought about it a few minutes and said I would with the understanding we would work in the same room, she wouldn't take a room and I another. He must have told her what I said.

The next day she drove out home to see me. Ed told her I was in the Laundromat in Canandaigua. She came and asked me if I was willing to work with her. I told her "yes, under the conditions I had told Mr. Dewey." She went up to the Welfare Office and resigned. I was happy to hear that, she and I would never have worked together very long.

I worked three years at the Monroe County Hospital. Two of those years I was on 3B Division which was the men's surgical floor. Everyone had to take a month each year on either the 3:00 to 11:00 or 11:00 to 7:00 shift. You could volunteer or the Supervisor would assign you. I chose P.M.s during the winter month as I drove from home to Henrietta Rd. The winter months were the hardest. I could have a room in the nurses' home for $7.00 a month. We bought tickets for our meals. I had a hot plate in my room and had breakfast and lunch in my room. Going on duty at 3:00 PM I ate in the dining room at 6:00 and midnight. Esther came to work in the kitchen and became assistant cook soon. She had had experience as cook at Brigham Hall. She got more pay than I did, she deserved it.

Then the Supervisor thought I would like to work in Out Patient Department. I went, but the only thing I liked about it was I had a chance to read patient histories and results of autopsies. I worked there a year. They had more help there than anywhere else.

I then went back to the V.A. in Canandaigua for a while. It was when Dr. Liu was there doing neurosurgery. That was an all new experience for me. It was a new experience for most of the R.N.'s. I had the advantage as Dr. Liu supposed they had been trained in that branch of nursing, but most hadn't. Some had had no experience with mental patients.

I remember two special episodes. There was one doctor on Ward 1D who disliked one particular Japanese girl, June, who had chosen nurses training rather than be shipped to California to a concentration camp during WWII. She was working on our shift 3:00 to 11:00 and we had a very mean patient from 3B (violent ward). He was running a very high temperature and refused to eat or drink. They were tube feeding him every other day. They had a new antibiotic they were going to try on him. The doctor ordered June to give him the first capsule. She tried, but was unable to get it down him. She came to me and said she had to go to supper but if the doctor called, tell him she would try again when she came back. He called and asked if Miss "Hirohito" had given the patient his capsule. I told him what June had told me to tell him and he said "Why don't you give it to him, Mrs. Repard". No practical nurses were recognized and could give no meds; I was recognized only as an aid. I was surprised and asked if he really meant it. Jim Scanlan and I had been talking, wondering how it would go if we treated this patient the way he treated us. When the doctor said for me to give the capsule I told Jim we could try our method. Everyone else working thought we had gone mad. Jim got a pitcher of cold water, I got the patient's tray and we went in his room. Jim kicked the door shut and yelled "Open your mouth" and swore a blue streak, just like the patient did. It surprised the patient so he opened his mouth and Jim threw the capsule in the back of his mouth and poured three glasses of water down him, swearing at the top of his voice all the time. Then he told me to feed him his supper. I fed him his entire tray and he didn't cause any trouble. The next day when I went in the office the dotor asked what method I had used, they hadn't had any trouble feeding him or giving medicine that day. I said "You won't find our method in Miss Post's book of etiquette. He didn't ask for any more explanation. June went to Monterey Park, California when she finished. I had several letters from her after.

The second was with the other Japanese girl, Melba. She and June arrived at the V.A. at the same time. Melba was a tiny little girl who was Dr. Liu's favorite O.R. nurse. One day they were very short of help and after she got through in the O.R. at 3:00 PM they asked her to work 3:00 to 11:00 on 1D Surgical Ward. That was the ward I was assigned to most of the time. At that time I was going to the main dining room to eat supper. When I got back to the ward I went into the office and Melba was crying, the medicine cabinet doors wide open, the whole ward in general uproar. Another patient, a very difficult man, about 75 years old, was yelling at the top of his lungs "She tried to kill me." I asked her what had happened and she said she had given him Lysol instead of Elixir Cofronhydrate a cough medicine. She said she was going to turn herself in, that she wasn't fit to be a nurse, etc. I ran into the kitchen a beat up the white of an egg and milk and gave it to the old patient. He vomited and I was sure she had made the mistake because of the strong Lysol odor. I got the emesis basin and took it in the men's toilet and emptied it, washed the basin leaving no odor. The old man quieted down and I went into the office and shut the door. I told her I wasn't going to let her turn herself in as she was just about ready to take her state board exams, and I knew they wouldn't let her if she reported herself. I talked to her, telling her I was sure there never was a nurse who hadn't made a mistake of some kind and she would be a better nurse for having made one. The dose was only one dram. She wasn't aware that internal medicines were kept on the upper shelves and external on the bottom shelves. She had half the medicine bottles out of the cabinet. The shelves were glass and dusty enough so I could set each bottle back in its own track. I then locked the cabinet and gave her the keys. It was very much against the rules that I even had the keys which I had picked up off the floor. It would not have happened if she had been used to working the wards. It was lucky Dr. Chaffee was O.D. that night. After she quieted down I let her call the O.D. He wanted to know what had occurred; I told him she was upset because she had given the wrong medication. He was very nice and said if it would make her feel better he would lavage (clean out) Charlie's stomach. He did and said he didn't find any evidence of Lysol, I was sure he wouldn't. After a while Mrs. Kilpatrick, an elderly R.N. who had asthma so badly it took her a long time to get around to all the wards, said she had heard about it before she got on the ward. She said "I don't want to hear another word". She was very out of breath. I am sure it was written up on the O.D.'s report. Melba had gone to the nurses' home at 11:00 but was up at 7:00 AM for the O.R. She met me at the elevator as I came to work the next day at 3:00 and asked "Do you know what Mrs. Funk said?" Mrs. Funk was the Charge nurse, not very popular. Mrs. Funk had told Melba that should teach her not to get upset at what a patient like that old man said. Melba was greatly relieved. After she graduated I heard she was working in a Denver V.A. O.R. I believe she worked there until she retired.

There was a family, in 1935, which lived in a tenant house on the farm of "Grut" Chapin. He worked for $3.00 a week. His wife had her third baby. The Welfare system was just being set up in this county. The cost of delivery in the hospital was high. I am not sure but somewhere near $100.00. The head of the system wanted to make a name for himself, so he experimented by sending her home without lunch. Dr. Howard asked me to go over and take care of the baby (not including anything else). I got there and such a desolate place. The county nurse brought the patient and baby home, arrived just a few minutes after noon, the husband had gone back to work. After learning she had had no lunch I went looking. In the pantry was a half pint jar of cooked string beans. I went out and looked in the chicken coup and found an egg. There was not a dish in the house that didn't leak. The county nurse was there yet and suggested I make a list of things needed. Did I ever make a list, nothing but what was needed. Sheets and pillow cases, hand clothes (bath and dish), night gown, it was summer time. I sent for table dishes and cooking utensils, soap and baby clothes. There were no diapers in sight. The welfare head was demoralized. I think it was the last of his experiments. There was one real nice thing. After I got a broom I swept the kitchen and the dirt fell down between the boards of the floor. I stayed the rest of the day as the mother was deaf. Later that year they moved to a house at the end of our road where Leonard went to school, after the school house burned. That was the year Ed had thirteen acres of tomatoes and after the canning factory stopped taking them the ground was red with ripe tomatoes. He told them they could have as many as they wanted. He gathered bushels and bushels of tomatoes and she canned them. They bought macaroni with their welfare money. The mother had a broken coccyx bone at the end of her spine and had to have surgery. When they went to the hospital they stopped and asked me to keep the baby while he took her to the hospital. After they left my mother asked "Why can't I keep the baby while she's in there?" I called the mother on the phone at the hospital and she gladly gave her consent, and then cried on the phone. Mom became very attached to the baby and cried when they took him back. By that time their other children had returned. They lived on macaroni and tomatoes that year. The next spring he got a job on a farm in Brockport and we never heard from them again.

There was another case in that same house. The family had moved to this county from another county and was not eligible for welfare. I can't remember how many children but they were expecting another. One of the older children had an ulcerated tooth and they had asked Dr. Howard to go down and see to that. Then Dr. Howard called me and asked me if I'd like to do a little charity work. I went there and was amazed. She was washing on a board and said she had just been able to get a bar of soap. It was desolate. Nearly Christmas, as Sunday school it was discussed that our class help. We gathered together some things we didn't need and the Sunday school class had a party and Ed and I went and took what we had to give. Everyone had a contribution.

The next Sunday the committee announced they had counted that family out as one woman had heard the father refused to do chores for .30 a day. Me and my big mouth said I had as much respect for the man who refused it as I did for the man who offered it. Mrs. Eghert said .30 a day would have at least bought bread. When I told my mother she devised her own system. We had just sold our roasters and seven had escaped. They killed three of them and she cooked them, made bread, pies, cookies, and vegetables and packed them up. We scrounged around and got more clothes. One of the neighbors gave all her baby clothes and outgrown things,. We sent Ed up to give them the things. He was pretty upset when he came back; he said the kids were eating breakfast, pancakes with nothing on them. We later heard that at Halloween time this woman heard the school was serving graham crackers and hot chocolate. She took the kids and walked to school. She had no coat and the Wheeler girl gave her a sweater she had worn to school.

Dr. Howard told me to forget delivering the baby at home; he was taking her to the hospital and let them worry about how they were to be paid. That house has been torn down a long time ago.

In 1935 I remember a special case. A prostitute had been arrested in a hotel in Geneva. She had done an abortion on herself and was bleeding badly. The State Troopers called the Welfare Supervisor for permission to take her to F.F. Thompson Hospital. I imagine they did a D&C on her and put her in the women's ward. That ward had eight beds separated by curtains. A patient in the next bed to her had company one P.M., I think it was her husband. The curtains were drawn, but this patient pulled the curtain back and tapped the visitor on the shoulder. He looked back and she lay perfectly naked. He was insulted and reported it to the supervisor. I believe the patient had been there a few days; the Supervisor called Welfare Supervisor and said they couldn't keep her any longer. I remember distinctly this occurred on Saturday PM and I was hurrying to get my work done as I was to be off Sunday. She was brought out to the County Home and I was told to give her a County night gown and house coat and take her clothes and lock them up. This was one of the episodes that brought me to quit that job. The Welfare Supervisor's wife ordered me to give her clothes back to her. I felt that the Welfare Supervisor was trying to avoid further trouble and I was more than busy, so I ignored her request. She ordered the people in the dining room to serve this girl's meals on a tray in her room. At that time inmates had tin cups and plates. The patient refused the tray so Welfare Supervisor's wife took the girl over to her own house and put her in her daughter's bed. After the M.D. examined her he decided she had a venereal disease. I had to go over to the house and give her a shot (hypo) of milk every day. That was supposed to relieve pain. Welfare Supervisor's wife catered to that girl every possible way. They took her to Rochester and bought her new clothes, two suitcases full. They baked the day before she was to leave and packed a lunch for her to take with her. She promised to return to a home of a Molly Green somewhere in South Carolina. They took her to the train. They never heard from her after. They telegraphed to a city she was supposed to change trains. They were told she left train number 1 but no one had any knowledge of where she went from there.

There were many such episodes where I was caught in the middle. After several I resigned, a very stressful time. There were many write-ups in the Messenger about what a wonderful person Welfare Supervisor's wife was. I guess I wasn't as nice as I couldn't take all the foolishness that went on from time to time. Funny I forgot her name.

A Poem to Aunt Edna
by Evelyn Richmond

I missed another chance today
To travel over Holcomb way.
To take the time to go and see
Someone who means a lot to me.

I missed the chance to go and talk
To chat along a memory walk.
To have the past come real again
When we were kids and so young then.

I missed the chance to sit and hear
The tales of those whom I hold dear.
About my Grandma when she was small,
Where she lived and played and all.

I missed the stories of our misdeeds,
When some would follow and one would lead.
Of playing hide and seek behind the bales,
And telling sad and scary tales.

I missed the chance to look on thru,
Family pictures, both old and new.
To hear the news of distant cousins,
The ones who were cheaper by the dozen.

I missed the chance to feel the care,
To shelter in the love that's there.
But I'll not miss this time to tell,
My Dear Aunt Edna, I Love You Well.

Meditation on the Life of Edna Evalyn Repard

A eulogy by unknown author.

The primary word that comes to mind when Edna Evalyn Repard's name is mentioned is family. For family was primary for Edna and all the Repards and Richmonds as well. And family meant in the richest, fullest, best-lived sense, not in the sense of all the politically-motivated uses of that word in the last decade. For this family is not only large in numbers, it is large in their sense of heritage, genealogy, and history; large in their understanding of relationships, large in their practice of hospitality and care, large in their inclusion of others, large in their acceptance of diversity, large in their love of life and laughter, large in their appreciation of a life lived long and well, as was Edna's.

Edna was born in Phelps in 1903. Her dad was a farmer, but one who moved around a lot building barns, and working on the railroad. Indeed, his work on the railroad eventually led to his meeting a young man named Ed Repard, who would be the man Edna married. But before that happened, she had gone off to live at a doctor's hospital in Rochester, to study to become a nurse. That school later became known as Park Ave. Hospital School of Nursing. Edna became an LPN; in fact, one of the very first ones in the whole state of New York. I believe she told me the number on her license was 6, meaning she was one of the first 10 LPN's in this state. She spent most of her life as a nurse, both within and without the hospitals she served, working until she was 72, only stopping then because her mother was ill and needed health care at home — so, in a real sense she didn't really stop even then.

One of her nursing tasks was to help deliver babies, and she did that all over this area, usually getting there before the doctor and usually doing most of the work, even though the doctor got the $5 payment. She not only delivered the babies, but would then stay with the new mom for a week to care for her and the little one. I met one of those mom's last night who spoke of Edna's care some sixty years ago at the birth of her son.

She then worked at the VA Hospital, usually with the psych patients, whom she treated with dignity and respect even though most did not. Because of this, she was far more successful at getting the patients to calm down, or respond better than the other workers. She also worked at the County Hospital and her oldest two boys, Jim and Rod, remember going and staying there with her when she had to stay there on occasions.

Yet her nursing wasn't limited to delivering babies and hospitals. She constantly had to patch up her boys and all the neighbor's kids when they got cut, scratched, or otherwise bruised and broken. Her use of Watkins Petro-Carbo Salve is legendary -- she used it for all kinds of sores and wounds, and most everyone in the family still swears by it to this day.

But in spite of all this great nursing practice and experience, she once felt a pain of her own she thought might be a gall stone. She went to the doctor and told him that. He said, "Well, Edna, it isn't a gall stone; you're pregnant." And Jake (Jerry) became the child thought to be a gall stone. She took a lot of kidding about her nursing skills then, and Jake has been a kidder ever since.

Edna was very fascinated with genealogy. She traced her heritage back on her father's side to du Richmond, who accompanied William the Conqueror into England, and now her granddaughter, Amy, lives in Richmond, VA, named after one of those Richmond descendants, I believe. Her interest in genealogy lives on in others of the family. Edna had a sense of people and place, recently telling Jim all the names of all the families on all the farms on the road where she grew up. It is a sense that kept her in the same house for nearly 80 years, a house that has seen five generations of Repards.

Edna was always kind and forgiving, having learned from her mother and father, and put into practice, a grand tolerance and acceptance of all kinds of people — different races and colors, and people of poor resources, or even bad reputations. She learned to help whoever was in need and was very generous in doing so, listening to them as well as helping them, in her gentle, caring, nurturing way. She always wanted to be useful, helpful with something to do, and if she wasn't busy, she'd try to help someone who was. Yet she could also be quite forceful and direct when she thought it necessary, never hesitating to tell you what she thought. And if you needed your behind dusted off a bit, she could do that, too, remembers Jake.

Edna was a great teller of tales and stories of all her experiences and family members have many fond memories of her doing that. She always remembered the cute little things about the kids and grandkids. She was an avid reader -- history, biography, philosophy -- all kinds of books of substance. She once read a huge textbook-like book about the South, gave it to Amy to read, but Amy says it was much too difficult to get through for her. She was very aware of world events, reading papers, watching the news and loved to talk about it, though she would often add, "I don't know why I do; there's nothing I can do about it." She loved the TV show Jeopardy and rarely missed the evening version. There wasn't much she didn't know or observe.

Her life and love of life while helping others lives on in her three sons, nine grandchildren, and nine great-grandchildren. It is obvious this is so by the wonderfully warm and open telling of her life story by the family. Their love for her, her love in them is obvious and will last their lifetimes. For this is a large family in its life and love and I have been privileged to have heard their stories, and been blessed by their presence.